The

APOCALYPSE

SURVIVAL

GUIDE

to your APOCALYPSE SURVIVAL KIT

The "Ready for Anything" Edition

Julio E. Pizarro

ISBN-13: 978-1979564403

ISBN-10: 197956440X

No interns were harmed in the making of this guide, but if they were, we would have disposed of all the bodies responsibly.

INTRODUCTION

The following guide contains all the stuff you need to have in your Apocalypse Survival Kit (ASK) and why you'll probably die horribly if you don't.

This guide focuses on the essentials, meaning what you can fit into just one bag.

This guide is the result of extensive and pain staking research performed on interns, ex-employees, and assorted office jerks with poor break room etiquette.

Though we strive for accuracy and comprehensiveness, every apocalyptic situation is different so please don't sue us if we leave something out ...oh wait, when the apocalypse comes you can't.

That makes our work pretty awesome.

Still, if it makes you feel any better, when an apocalypse comes we'll be out there following our Apocalypse Survival Guide just like you.

CONTENTS

STUFF YOU NEEDED ANYWAY

Water

One of the main killers of our survival test subjects is lack of water. Studies have proven conclusively that pasty mouths quickly lead to moaning complaints which can sound a lot like the moans of the infected. This can attract vultures and scavengers from miles around so stay hydrated and give your co-survivors one less reason to up their own personal share of the rations.

Water Pouches

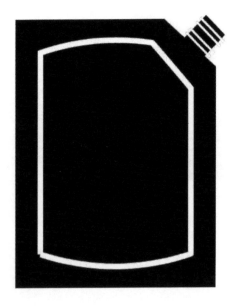

What is your number one survival requirement?

Air.

A close second comes not killing yourself, and right behind that is keeping all your limbs attached, but somewhere in the top 50 we can assure you is water.

Some animals can smell it from miles away but if you're still human then you won't have the first clue so put away the dousing rod and just pack your own water instead.

Survival tips you'll thank us for:

Survival water is not recommended for water balloon fights, free car washes, pissing contests, or bartering for anything other than guns and ammo; which of course could immediately pay for itself.

Water Purification Tablets

We have two words for you, 'projectile vomit'.

If you're not convinced yet here are 4 more, 'peeing from your butt'.

Water is the basis for life on this planet but that isn't a good thing when your next glass of water is teeming with life, all of which are hell-bent on taking yours.

Duct tape

Duct tape, and water? What? Are they crazy? Nope.

Your hands leak like a three year old with a secret they've sworn on *your* life never to tell. Duct tape those mitts of yours into a bowl, or just make a survival water bag out of duct tape; then brag obnoxiously for weeks about how you'll be the last of your survival buddies to die.

Air

What's better than coating the insides of your lungs with the irradiated ashes of your former life? Just about anything else we can think of.

So keep a dust mask or bandana handy and go find yourself a more pleasant way to die.

Dust Mask

Not only might a dust mask keep you from breathing in virus ridden plague juice; it also looks intimidating.

The next time raiders come, just put this on, grab a machete and chop up your own survival buddies while singing opera at the top of your lungs. Those raiders just might think you're crazy enough to leave alone and you just might end up with the most undisturbed survival outpost in the wasteland.

Your late survival buddies would have been so proud of you.

Duct Tape

You can use duct tape to make a ball and preserve some air for emergencies. Of course if you blow it up yourself it will be filled with carbon dioxide but at least in an emergency your death should be painless.

Sleep well.

QUICK TIP:

What you don't see can kill you.

Food

Your co-survivors will get scrawny eating driveway gravel and tree bark. Lure them and all their meat using your vast stores of delicious survival food as bait. Just make sure to save actually eating those survival rations for the long lonely days ahead.

Energy bars

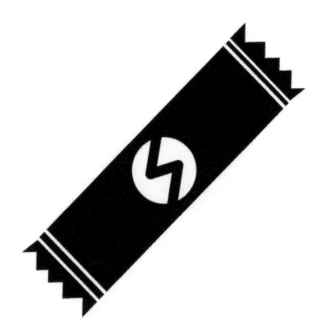

Go Fishing.

Few things will give away your location faster than a growling stomach. Conversely, few things will give away an enemy location like their growling stomachs. Just unwrap one of these nutritious puppies when you're trying to ferret out another half-starved survivor or rabid radioactive mutant bear, and you'll be sure to find them in no time.

Seeds

-- - --- - - ----- -- - --- - --- -

Let gullible co-survivors think you're a vegetarian by growing your own food. They won't even notice that you only grow side dishes and seasonings. Who says vegetarians can't get enough protein. Your garden will bring you an endless supply.

Remember, you are what you eat, and while those guys are barely human anymore, you still are, 100%.

Duct tape

Duct tape or bandanas could be used to keep food away from bears but more importantly while your survival mates are sleeping you can use it to muffle the sounds of you opening what just might be the last bag of chips in existence.

QUICK TIP:

What they don't know won't have to be shared with them.

Fire & Warmth

Fire is not for what you're thinking you little pyros, it's for food and warmth.

Our lab tests have repeatedly indicated that research assistants locked in a freezer will die if they can't get a fire going.

Our research has also shown that interns fed a diet of raw meat are either bursting at the seams (sometimes literally) with parasites, or they develop a taste for it.

Keep a fire going so your co-survivors never develop a taste for something you're made of.

Waterproof Matches

- -- -- ----- -- - --- --- - -- - -

Humans thought language use made us different from other animals; then we realized dolphins and bees use it.

Then we thought recognizing ourselves in the mirror made us different; then a crow proved us wrong.

Grasping at straws we thought war was solely a human thing; then chimps and ants proved us wrong.

Tool use? Nope.

Emotions? No luck there.

Still, there's one thing we've got that they haven't got. So light a match when that pack of hungry plague-wolves corners you and show them, for a few seconds at least, who's still top dog.

Emergency
Blanket

Some people out there call these Space Blankets. We think they'll all die pretty quickly.

We at the lab don't think that name is cool enough. This thing can keep you warm, and if your legs aren't too long, it will even keep you dry in the rain. We generally call it a Survival Blanket; but if that horribly mutated thing stalking you out there in the wastelands has heat vision, then you might just be calling this an Invisibility Cloak.

Now that's a cool name.

Full Body Warmer

Be prepared for anything that might come at you and keep your meat warm for zombies, cannibals, plague wolves... or all of the above.

If you're prepared for anything then your survival buddies will always regard you as the most valuable member of the group when the food runs out.

Rest & Shelter

Duct tape: It's how you make a shelter, it's how you keep your shelter, and it's probably the most important thing you'll put in your shelter; after you of course.

Pup Tent

Go ahead and let your survival friends laugh at your little pup tent. I bet it will only take a night or two spent eating a face full of acid rain before they come over to you with a burning desire to apologize.

Sleeping Bag

What's better than being asleep at night when a bunch of well-armed survivor jerks raid your camp? ...being 20 feet in the air in your duct tape-met-sleeping-bag-and-made-a-baby-hammock when a bunch of well-armed survivor jerks raid your camp.

Get a good night's rest while your soon-to-be former survival mates deal with the rude interruptions of raiders, aliens and radioactive mutants.

Poncho with Hood

Hooded cloaks can make you look dangerous and mysterious.

Colorful ponchos are more likely to make you look insane, which is even better.

Intimidate those would-be raiders from a distance and hope that they're low on bullets and fresh out of good aim.

Otherwise you'll just give them all a good story to tell, which is kind of the same as immortality isn't it?

Duct tape

-- - - -   - - -- - - - -- - - - -- - - -

How do you turn a stinking pile of garbage bags into a luxurious yurt?

Duct tape.

How do you keep the smell of your sweet uneaten flesh from slipping through the cracks of your new garden shed shelter and luring every zombie within sniffing distance?

Duct tape.

How do you tape newspapers all over your windows so your half dead survival neighbors don't see that you're living the good life with your Apocalypse Survival Kit?

Yeah, you get the idea.

Light

Do you know why they called the dark ages the dark ages? Yep, you guessed it, massive power outages for the whole country of Europe. And they stayed without power the whole time; stumbling about in the dark, stubbing toes, bumbling into dinosaurs and desperately calling out to each other like lonely wolves in the night.

Depressing.

Europeans wouldn't get to see the faces of their loved ones again for eons. No one wants their kids to grow up thinking their parents are just voices in their heads. Learn a thing or two from those hard lessons and pack some survival light; if for no other reason then for the sake of your unbroken toes, and maybe even for your uneaten-by-a-dinosaur-spleen.

Rechargeable
Squeeze Flashlight

Use it to read your apocalypse survival guide, to find stuff you dropped, to signal your survival friends, to navigate your survival pup tent, heck you can even attract a mate lightning bug style by flashing patterns into the night.

So what if they don't understand a word you're saying, you won't understand them either, and now the two of you have something in common.

QUICK TIP:

Yes there can be dating after the internet is dead and gone, but no you can't repopulate the world without a rechargeable survival squeeze flashlight handy.

Emergency Glow Stick

12 hour Emergency Glow Stick:

Around the lab we call them cave sticks since half the day you won't otherwise need one because of a little thing we call the sun.

24 hour Emergency Glow Stick:

What no sun? Just a sky full of serial murdering storm clouds or hellish molten debris that incinerated all vegetation? For months? Years even? You probably won't even notice with one of these 24 hour tiny day makers. Pack a picnic. It will be as if that whole apocalypse thing never even happened! At least until your buzzkill 12-hour-glow-stick-having survival buddies run out of their own glowshine and butterflies and come begging for some of yours.

30 Hour
Emergency Candle

- - -- - -- - --- - --- - -- - - --

What's better than light on a cold post-apocalyptic winter night? ... light and a little heat to go with it.

So grab a good Apocalypse Survival Guide to read, bundle up under your survival blanket, and hope that post-apocalyptic wind doesn't blow too hard.

QUICK TIP:

On a postapocalyptic diet you'll want to conserve energy but you don't want to get flabby; a squeeze flashlight achieves that delicate balance of exercise to keep you looking like an athlete.

Dynamo 4-in-1
Flashlight

1. A flash light to keep you from devolving into a protozoan,
2. a radio so you can brag about your flashlight to your co-survivors as they stumble about in the dark,
3. a siren to lure them in when you're feeling lonely or just hungry,
4. and a charger to remind you what technology used to look like just in case someone ever invents it again...

This doohickey has everything you need in order to keep yourself at the top of the evolutionary ladder; where you probably don't belong.

NOT DYING

First Aid Kit

A first aid kit isn't about treating cuts and sprains, it's about making yourself immune to everything.

Ever notice in movies that everyone calls for the medic but no one ever seems to blame them when the supporting characters die anyway. They don't even get blamed for not showing up! It's always just fade to black and on to the next scene as if nothing happened. We think it's like being a weatherperson where people keep tuning in no matter how many times the weatherperson's guesses are off the mark.

So bring a first aid kit everywhere you go, change your name to medic, and inoculate yourself from ever doing any wrong. Everything you do or don't do will evidently be forgiven, if they even notice. If anyone starts to think that they could carry the first aid kit and the distinction of medic because they saw the same movies as you, just keep using big words like faecal encephalopathy, cranio-intergluteal insertion, transient diaphragmatic spasm, rhinotillexomania, sphenopalatine ganglioneuralgia. If they correct your pronunciation of those terms just remember, [wink,wink] as the medic you can do no wrong.

Gloves

Removing pesky alien anal probes, cavity searching people wanting to join your new civilization, pulling rabid radioactive ticks from pustulating zombie bites..., gloves are your armor against the unpleasant jobs.

Yes those jobs still need to be done, but when you delegate the chore to those less valuable co-survivors, you can at least make them feel a tiny bit better about it

...because you're a good person.

Quick Tip:

What you don't know just might devour you from the inside out.

Burn Cream

-- -- -- - - -- -- - - -- - - -- --   - -

As your less prepared survival buddies die off one by one, leaving you their rations and meat, your remaining survival groupies are going to have a lot of cooking to do for your inevitable coronation feast and only survival foil to burn their fingers with while doing it.

Keep their nasty little peon blisters from touching your royal hand as they kneel to kiss your ring... your majesty.

QUICK TIP:

You should start thinking now about what to rename the wastelands when they declare you emperor.

Sunscreen

In our professional opinions, one of two things might happen:

A) You get caught out during the apocalypse in which case no amount of sunscreen will protect you from the radiation, flaming meteors, and rising heat as the earth heads straight into the sun. But it will provide you a bit of confidence which is precisely what you'll need to go out like a boss while everyone else loses their cool. As the masses huddle at your feet the moment before earth disintegrates and like a photo, its last light will head off into the infinite of space for an eternity, you'll leave a good last impression.

B) You manage to take shelter during the apocalypse and soon devolve into some cave dwelling atrocity desperately in need of sunscreen whenever you go hunting on the surface for hapless Eloi to devour.

Either way you look at it, you're going to need it.

Aspirin

-- --   -- --   --- --   -- --   --   - --- -- --   --

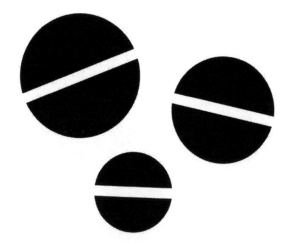

Got a fever? Hide that fact with aspirin. It might not even be the early onset of a mutation into a cannibalistic humanoid abomination, it could just be ebola, rabies, or the black plague; still those ingrate co-survivors will throw you to the plague wolves the minute you start getting just a little bit warm.

Sting Relief Cream

-- -- --- -- --- -- -- - ---

Don't be an ordinary leader of the wasteland, be a great one.

As throngs of survival groupies and other poor souls without their own ASK come begging to join your new civilization, likely the only civilization, you'll have to pick who gets in and who doesn't. When you say no to that guy that happens to remind you of some unrelated jerk that you didn't like in preapocalyptia, toss him some sting relief and make the ordinary sting of rejection a great big sting.

It's not because you're a jerk, it's because great leaders do great things.

Duct tape

Well how else are you supposed to stick them back together?

When you realize that human organs don't really snap together the way they did in biology class you'll find that duct tape is your patient's friend.

After playing doctor, duct tape will help keep all those bits and pieces from making a mess on the floor. How do you think hospitals keep their operating rooms so neat and clean?

Post-surgery you can even use duct tape to keep all those extra bits in one place until you figure out which person they came from and if those parts were even necessary in the first place.

QUICK TIP:

Our lab tests indicate a high probability that no one will come back to claim those extra parts.

PEOPLE NOT WANTING YOU TO DIE

Grooming & Hygiene

It's what we like to call "playing well with others."

Toothbrush &
Toothpaste

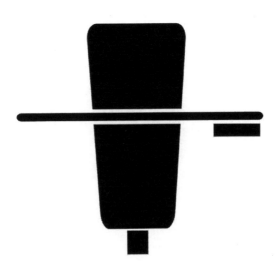

Teeth can be sharpened to make arrowheads, or to turn a boring club into an exciting spiked mace.

With a little skill and patience they can be carved and strung together to make a fabulous necklace.

You can even get musical and use those teeth to make maracas, leg rattles or guitar picks.

Or you can just brush your teeth, keep them in your head, and not have to make any of those other things in order to pay people to chew your food for you.

QUICK TIP:

Warning: If you haven't read the Grooming & Hygiene section before, then your survival buddies are probably only tolerating you because of your ASK.

Breath Mints

-- - -- ---- - -- -- - --- -

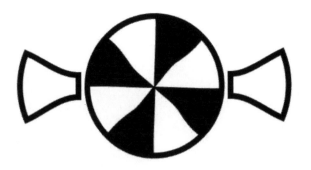

For your survival buddies that don't have their own toothbrushes. Breath mints won't save their teeth but they will give them minty fresh breath hours longer than your toothbrushing will. Train those lurking radiation mutant predators encircling your camp how to easily recognize those of you that can't bite back.

[Hint: they're the ones that still smell minty]

Now sit back and watch your share of the rations just grow and grow.

Soap

- - - - -   - - - -   - -   - -   - - -   - - - -   - - - - - -

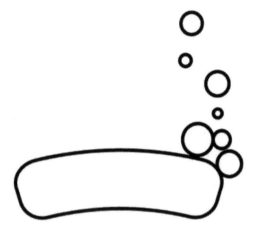

Test subjects always identified the cleanest member of the group as the one most likely to be the leader. So do raiders.

You can wallow in the mud to make yourself less of a target to invading survival raider jerks but that might mean risking some mud dwelling mutated parasites that no one has ever seen before. Why not just pass the soap to some more deserving target instead.

"Why thank you," they'll say.

And you'll say, "No..., thank you."

Tissues

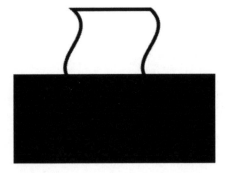

Now why in the world would tissues be vital to human survival?

To keep you from sneezing of course.

How many times have you and your fellow survivors been hiding from bandits, aliens, or mutated chipmunks? You found a good hiding spot and just when the bad guys are about to give up on finding you, somebody has to sneeze... If you had a Breath Mint for every time that happened, you'd only have one; think about it.

Moist Towelettes

- - --- - - -- -- --- - - -- -- -- - -- -- -

Strike terror into the hearts of others and become the stuff of nightmares by always keeping a moist towelette handy.

Let us explain:

Somewhere deep down each of us unconsciously remembers some mother figure gently caressing our bottoms with a comforting diaper wipe or warm soothing wash cloth as they protected our butts from a horrible disaster of our own making.

During the apocalypse, moist towelettes won't save you from any of the thousand, thousand things coming to get you. But as the inevitable closes in, you can pull out your not-so-survival moist towelette and die with a comforted smile on your face.

That means you can creep out all of your neighboring wasteland survivors as a smiling corpse, haunting them whenever they close their eyes.

Therefore, strike terror into the hearts of others and become the stuff of nightmares by always keeping a moist towelette handy.

Shaving Cream
and Razor

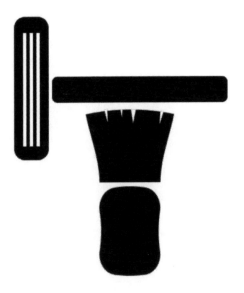

You don't need to be a biologist to see that evolution has been quietly shaving us more and more bald for millions of years.

As you and your survivor buddies return to your roots and start growing hair like a Sasquatch, why not shave your way back to the modern era and pretend that you still retain some of your former humanity.

Or you could shave it all off and pretend that you've evolved into something better.

QUICK TIP:

What they don't know won't hurt them until you get hungry enough.

Comb/Brush

String is one of the most useful things to have for survival crafting that you simply won't have in the apocalypse.

Start grooming your co-survivors and open a string factory using their hair. You'll corner the market early and soon be the wealthiest denizen of the wastes. You'll have more bulging cans of dog food, expired liver paste and jars of capers than you could possibly appreciate.

QUICK TIP:

We are so confident that this guide will help you to build a new civilization that we might even be personally counting on it.

Duct Tape

When one of your survival-mates-turned-yeti asks to borrow a shaving razor hand them some duct tape instead.

True there are quieter ways to shave but where's the fun in that?

CAREER TIP:

We at apocalypsesurvivalkit.com have immediate openings for lab assistants with a high tolerance to chemical burns, and experience with unshielded exposure to radioactive materials. Visit our career page to learn more.

CHOCK FULL
OF
POTENTIAL

Multi-Tools

These things are like the Duct tape of tools just without the sticky.

QUICK TIP:

It's nice to have choices.

Multi-Tool Survival Whistle

- -- -- - - - - -- -- -- - -- - -- -

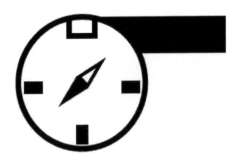

You can use this anywhere but our researchers recommend heading out to the open ocean.

Picture yourself setting out to sea on a roughshod raft; finding your way with your trusty compass; signaling passing pirates with your mirror; starting fires at night for warmth on your floating tinderbox; showing off your better fortunes by whistling at shipwreck survivors clinging pathetically to wood planks and toilet seats as they float past; or making friendship bracelets with your lanyard to lure in the meatiest of them.

Yes it all comes in a waterproof case because, especially during an apocalypse, there's nowhere on the planet that you shouldn't be able to go and be a jerk.

Multi-tool Knife

-- -- -- - ---- - - -   -- - - - - -

When the apocalypse comes and your crumby old life has burned to ash, you'll be starting a new one anyway so why not pick the one you want?

You can live out your debonair secret agent fantasies with only this one gadget.

It has tooth pick, tweezers, scissors, and a nail file so you can always look well-groomed and generally better than the survival slob next to you.

It has a hook disgorger, fish scaler, cap lifter, cork screw, and key ring because, as the owner of an Apocalypse Survival Kit, even in the apocalypse you'll be living the three aphrodisiacs, seafood & caviar, rare wine, and fast cars.

It has two screwdrivers, a reamer and a saw for getting out of villainous traps that would eventually kill you when no one is watching.

Lastly it has a blade because you're dangerous and now everyone will know it.

Multi-tool Shovel

We call this the "choose your next adventure tool".
Page one: You built a raft and you've been living like
a Viking and raiding coastal villages in the night. The
angry surviving locals have now built their own ship
and hunted you down. What do you do?

You could go to page 41 and use the saw, hammer,
and nails to help them rebuild their village so you'll
have something to raid again next year;

page 264 and use the fishing line, bobbers and hooks
to convince them that your just a fisherman out for a
pleasure cruise though mutant eel infested waters;

page 89 and use the compass to navigate your way to
an area where angry locals don't know how to build
ships;

page 25, use the wrench to turn your raft into a
submarine and then hope the radiation causes you to
mutate into something with gills so you can start a
new life under the sea;

or add your own page and just beat them all to death
with the hatchet edge of your shovel and bury the
evidence in the morning.

THE NEW NORMAL

Cover & Concealment

Some of the advice from the Art of War just doesn't translate well to the Art of Surviving.

Natural disasters don't care about your plans, zombies are too dumb to understand deception, and aliens are too smart to be outsmarted.

Sometimes you need to think a little outside of the kit in order to complete your kit.

Makeup Kit

- - - -- - -- -- - - -- - -- -- - -- -- --

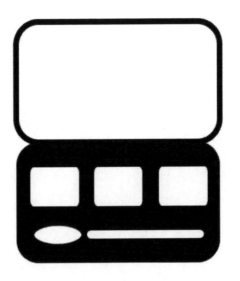

This probably isn't what you were thinking would go under Cover & Concealment but we have some relevant observations to report here.

Want to have that survival shelter all to yourself? Do yourself up to look like you have never before seen symptoms and infectious sores, and then chase everyone else out of what will become your newly private one person hideout.

Semblance of Order

When the world goes to crap in a car with recalled brakes, you'll long for a sense of order and normalcy. So will everyone else.

But who needs order when you can have the semblance of it for half the work? Restoring order is hard, but making it look that way can be easy!

With the following gear you can give them something to thank you for without all of the effort.

Ententainment

Grab a deck of cards and make some extra bottle caps telling fortunes. You already know how it's going to end for anyone without an ASK guide so at least you'll get a reputation for accuracy.

QUICK TIP:

Here's a game you can play:

What's for dinner?

It's just like old maid except the person who loses in the end is the next person you and the other survivors get to... um..., yeah.

Pen and Paper

Record your experiences so others get to learn from your mistakes; or just lie about your experiences because if you're going down you might as well take as many with you as you can.

We won't tell.

CAREER TIP:

Are you homozygous for valine in your PRNP gene? If so, then find out more about our short term employment opportunities at apocalypsesurvivalkit.com.

Sewing Kit

-- -- --   -- -   -   -- - -- -

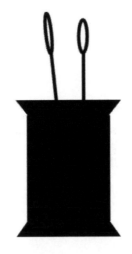

What's the difference between a "butcher of the wasteland" that everyone will pay good amounts of cat food and only mildly irradiated rat meat to have killed, and a "butcher of the wasteland" that everyone will pay good amounts to see?

A sewing kit.

So be the good kind of butcher and start your own medical practice.

Remember, all those left over parts, you get to keep. Think of it as a tip for your service to those less fortunate.

Duct Tape

-- -- -- --- --- -- -- --- -- --- -

Seriously, hygiene is one of the most important things you can practice in the apocalypse, so duct tape those hands of yours and keep them in preapocalyptic shape.

Of course it will be like wearing baseball mitts instead of surgical gloves for everything you do in your survival community, but then again, it's not like you knew what you were doing anyway. Plus, when anyone asks who screwed something up, you can show them that your hands are as clean as your conscience.

BACK TO BASICS

Tarp

Make a tent by holding up your tarp using survival rope, survival sticks or just a small handpicked selection of your countless survival groupies. Oh yeah, you'll have plenty of those as the proud owner of an Apocalypse Survival Kit.

Tarps can also be used to make a burrito style sleeping bag that will make your co-survivor's mouths water.

How about a makeshift stretcher so your lazy survival mates have fewer reasons to leave you behind when you twist your delicate ankle?

Use it as a billboard so you can put up a huge sign saying FREE FRESH SURVIVAL MEAT as a way of attracting some.

Garbage Bags

Garbage bags are a handy place for cowardly co-survivors to hide their heads in when they're too scared to go rescue you.

Just take a whole bunch of deep breaths and relax buddy.

Rope

You can also use rope to tie up your friends when they turn on you, or before they get to that point just in case. Just remember who history is written by; and if you're the only one with a free hand to write with...

Carrying and Storage

Camouflage Bags

What do zombies, raiders, aliens and roaming packs
of savage dogs blinded by starvation all have in
common? Your answer should be that they're not
color blind, and if it wasn't, then you might as well
be seasoning yourself for the reckoning.

So as you enjoy your camo bag, feel free to feel bad
for the suckers who got those bright orange or bright
red dinner bells they call survival packs.

Survival Pack

While your friends with the camo bags are
accidentally getting shot by unwitting hunters or by
their own friends (a.k.a. you), rest easy knowing that
while you trudge through the wilderness, anyone
looking down a scope can easily distinguish you from
the other meat. And if you're the friend who
accidentally shoots a camo wearing survivor buddy,
you still get to come home as the hero who increased
everyone's rations. Thanks camo guy.

Bandana

A bandana is the luxury version of duct tape. They are great for those few things that duct tape can probably do but shouldn't. Things like: sweatbands, cleaning and drying, anything (at all) to do with hair, lovely doilies, dusk masks (unless you're into shaving the manliest way possible), toilet paper, and even blowing your nose (but not in that order).

Duct tape can do it all, but sometimes you'll want that soft luxurious touch of cloth as opposed to the birthmark removing, hair pulling, skin thinning peel of duct tape -- but only sometimes.

Aluminum Foil

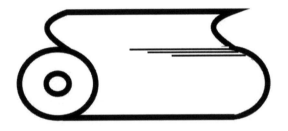

Foil can be used for making all kinds of things like pots and cooking aids, lures, light reflected signals to survivors in other buildings so you don't have to leave the safety of yours (which is what we meant by "lures"). If that works, you can even use it to help you store all the extra survival meat you're going to end up with as a result of having once had neighbors.

Toilet Paper

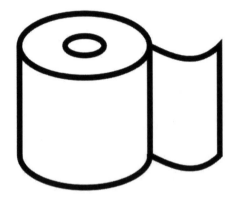

With only the addition of a little water, you can explore the limitless world of toilet papier-mâché.

Nose plugs: As your co-survivors revert to filthy stinking primitive versions of their already limited humanity, save your moist towelettes and just make nose plugs instead.

Earplugs: Get a good nap while those inconsiderate survival mates of yours are making a racket by rudely building fortifications or obnoxiously fending off invaders... yet again; so rude of them.

Butt plug: Stop those anal probes dead in their tracks (well your tract at least). If nothing else you can buy yourself some time to try and negotiate an intergalactic peace treaty. Just remember, it's your butt on the line.

And yes, "plugs" are multipurpose. Hey, it's the apocalypse; don't get squeamish on us now.

If you have no imagination then you could always use it for what it was designed for, the universal cure for skid marks in your underwear. Even an anal probing alien can appreciate that. Heck, maybe that's all they were in there looking for in the first place.

139

Duct tape

You can use duct tape for a first aid cast, a splint, a sling, as sutures, or as a makeshift sewing kit. It can even be used as a cup, a bowl, or a container. Consider its use as jewelry, clothing, as fashionable underwear, or make neckties, sandals, holsters for that gun you pretend to have, or as a bandolier to make you look more dangerous than you really are.

Duct tape can be used to make almost everything in your kit, or more importantly, to make everything in your kit even better.

You may even need to consider a duct tape based economy.

QUICK TIP

The only thing everyone absolutely needs to know about duct tape is that it is really noisy when you pull a piece off. You have been warned.

ASK Guide

Yep, your indispensable Apocalypse Survival Guide to your Apocalypse Survival Kit. Once you've committed it to memory and it has become an oral tradition for the future generations of your horribly mutated progeny, you can use it for all sorts of things.

You can swat the flies that gather to feast on those poor co-survivors without an ASK.

Keep an oppressive ledger of all the times others have asked you for something that you were prepared with and they weren't.

Keep track of the betting pool for how quickly and how gruesomely each of your unprepared survival buddies are going to perish.

You can even burn it for the warmth that comes from knowing that no one else can read it and become as valuable a member of your survival community as you are; their one and only Apocalypse Survival Guide.

"If we ASK you, are you prepared? What will you say?"